The Toilet Trained Cat

The Toilet Trained Cat

HOW TO TRAIN YOUR CAT TO USE THE HUMAN TOILET

... AND NEVER SCOOP LITTER AGAIN

ASTON LAU

For my loving fiancée, who supported my crazy dreams of toilet training our cat, put up with my experimentation, and helped clean up the accidents. I love you more than words can express.

"I simply can't resist a cat, particularly a purring one. They are the cleanest, cunningest, and most intelligent things I know, outside of the girl you love, of course."
—MARK TWAIN

Contents

❶

Why Toilet Train a Cat?

There is, incidentally, no way of talking about cats that enables one to come off as a sane person.
—DAN GREENBERG

When I tell people that I toilet train cats, the responses I get are mixed. Am I referring to litter training, or actual *human* toilets? And am I joking, or am I serious, and therefore certifiably insane?

To clarify, this book is all about teaching a cat to use an honest-to-goodness human toilet, the kinds that flush. We won't be making any crazy modifications to the toilet, either—no special mini toilet seats involved, no keeping litter in the toilet somehow, etc. The goal is to show you, step-by-step, how to train your cat to use a regular old toilet for pee and poop—and to save you from the tyranny of having to scoop the litter box every day.

Can a Cat Even Be Trained?

To be sure, I get my fair share of skeptics. Cats can't be trained because they're too stubborn and independent, right? Well, let me assure you, cats *can* be trained. Yes, they're independent creatures and some of them can be stubborn as heck... but, they also crave rewards such as treats, praise, and love, and we can use these rewards as incentives to get them to do what we want.

Of course, if you want definitive proof that cats can be trained to do #1 (pee) and #2 (poop) in the human toilet, just go to www.toilettrainedcat.com and watch the videos of my own cat, Miki, using the toilet all on her own. Training a cat *can* be done, and it's actually not that difficult... the only reason more cats aren't trained is because most people automatically assume that they can't be trained.

Why Toilet Train a Cat in the First Place?

If you're sitting on the fence, unable to decide whether to toilet train or not, here are just a few great reasons why you should consider it:

- **Convenience:** Compare cleaning out a litter box each day with pushing the handle on your toilet—as far as convenience goes, there's really no contest. If you teach your cat to flush, too, then you don't even have to push the handle.

- **Money:** You save at least $175 per year per cat on litter.[1] You save even more if you usually buy the expensive brands.

---

[1] Source: *ASPCA Pet Ownership Costs.*

http://www.aspca.org/flash/petcarecosts/petcarecosts.swf

- **Cleanliness:** Having a toilet trained cat eliminates the litter box odors in your home.

- **Environment:** Eliminating the litter box is better for the environment, since waste is flushed and filtered out of sewage by water treatment plants, instead of being dumped in our landfills. Contrary to popular belief, cat litter is **not** biodegradable, and each year over 4 billion pounds of it end up in landfills throughout the U.S.[1]

  Not only that, but clay (the main ingredient of litter) is strip mined, destroying soil and vegetation and leaving the land virtually useless for future use.

- **Health:** Using a toilet is better for your health as well as your cat's. Bacterial waste and silica dust created by a litter box can cause health problems for all of the living creatures in your household.

  Also, you may be aware that pregnant women should stay away from litter boxes. The reason for this is toxoplasmosis, a rare but serious parasitic disease that affects fetuses and people with weak immune systems. Cats are the primary hosts for this parasite, since cats excrete the pathogen in their feces.

  Removing the litter box from your home means that no humans have to be exposed to cat waste, eliminating this potential health risk.

---

[1] Source: Swheat Scoop® website.
http://swheatscoop.com/prcompost.html

- **Hygiene:** Being toilet trained is much more hygienic for the cat, as well as all of the humans in the household. Obviously, not having to clean the litter box each day is a major hygiene plus for you.

  Not only that, but the litter box itself is a toxic dump in your home. Think of all the time your cat currently spends tromping around in it, and then goes walking around your house, your couch, your kitchen counters, your bed, on you... it's not a pleasant thought!

Isn't Sharing a Toilet With a Cat Unhygienic?

Actually, when you think about it, it's probably more unhygienic to have your cat use a litter box, for the reasons cited above. You don't want your cat to walk around the house with her dirty, litter-stained paws! The litter box is easily the biggest source of germs in your cat's environment.

A toilet, on the other hand, is specially designed to deal with waste in the most hygienic way possible—by immersing it in water to reduce odors, and then flushing it away to be treated in water treatment plants.

Take away the litter box, and instantly you remove the biggest source of germs in your cat's life. In its place, your cat gets a clean toilet, and keeps her paws nice and spotless.

Isn't This Unnatural? Won't I Traumatize My Cat?

If you're worried that you'll traumatize your cat if you toilet train her, or you think it's just unnatural for a cat to use the toilet, consider this: is it any more natural for a cat to go in the same plastic litter box filled with chemically-scented clay litter over and over? Outdoor cats and cats in the wild naturally use the great outdoors as their litter box, and rarely use the same

Figure 1 *Miki digs in her old unhygienic litter box. Later, she will spread litter box germs all over my house*

spot twice... in fact, an outdoor domestic cat may range up to a mile from home in her daily travels, providing a lot of space to use for potty.

Moreover, cats like a clean place each time they do their business, and teaching a cat to use the toilet means a clean place to use each time, which may actually be *more* natural to use than a cramped litter box.

Will My Cat Fall Into the Toilet?

It's very unlikely—cats are exceptionally agile. Balancing and navigating on a toilet seat is an extremely simple task for a creature that bounds over fences and climbs trees for fun. There *are*

Figure 2 *Miki demonstrates her sense of balance by doing #2 on the toilet*

cats out there who are very small, overweight, or simply have poor balance, and if you suspect that your cat falls into one of these categories, you can make the toilet easier to use by providing a stool to make it easier to get up onto the toilet, as well as installing a wooden or padded toilet seat to allow your cat to get a better grip. (More on this later in the "Training Equipment" chapter.)

Will I Be Able to Use the Toilet During the Training Process?

Yes, you will, and you don't have to worry about throwing off your cat's training. The toilet training method described in this book involves putting a pan full of litter in the toilet bowl (this acts as your cat's litter box during the training process). All a human needs to do is remove the pan before they use the toilet. After the cat has been toilet trained, the pan and litter will be removed entirely, and the cat will know how to use a regular, unmodified toilet.

❷

Know Thy Cat, As Well As Thyself

When I play with my cat, how do I know that she is not passing time with me rather than I with her?
—Michel de Montaigne (1533-1592)

There are a number of things you'll need to consider before diving into toilet training your cat. I know you're itching to start training right away, but don't skip this part—these are important points you need to know before starting with the actual training process.

Can *My* Cat Be Trained?

The short answer is *yes*. Just about any cat can be trained to use the human toilet, no matter if the cat is unintelligent, stubborn, out of shape, or what have you. Of course, if your cat is intelligent, adaptable, and fit, she'll probably pick it up that much quicker, but it's not a requisite for training. There are, however, a couple of exceptions that you should be aware of.

Young Cats and Old Cats

If you have a very young kitten, you'll need to wait until she's a little older and using the litter box on her own. Wait until she's about 6 months old, and make sure she has enough balance and agility to jump onto the toilet seat. It's easy to test—simply pick her up and put her on the toilet seat (and spot her to make sure she doesn't fall in!). If you want to make sure she's able to jump up onto the seat on her own, get a treat and wave it over the toilet—that should get her hopping up onto the seat in a hurry. If she's having trouble with it, try placing a good sturdy stool beside the toilet, so that she can use it as an intermediate step instead of jumping up onto the toilet seat directly.

Conversely, if you have an older adult cat, then it may be difficult for you to toilet train. In theory, there's no upper age limit for training, and I've trained cats as old as 15 years old. However, older cats are more entrenched in their familiar potty habits, and the older they are, the harder it will be to break those habits and make them learn new ones. Personality types vary greatly between individual cats, though, so even though your cat may be ten or twelve or fifteen, she may be a genius and pick it up right away. Generally though, the older the cat, the longer it will take to toilet train.

Fat Cats and Cats With Poor Balance

Most cats have excellent balance and agility, so this shouldn't be a problem... but, if your cat is pleasantly plump to the point that it prevents her from being able to balance on the toilet, you may not be able to train her. There's no harm in trying, though—if it turns out that she's able to perform the balancing squat necessary to use the toilet, then great; if not, well, at least you tried. Nothing ventured, nothing gained!

Make Sure Your Cat is Already Litter-Trained

Aside from your cat's age and fitness level, it's also important to make sure your cat has gotten the hang of using the litter box first.

If your cat isn't properly litter-trained or has problems using the litter box consistently, choosing instead to do her business in inappropriate places, you'll need to fix this first. If you attempt to toilet train a cat who's not litter trained, hoping to magically fix her potty behavior (no pun intended), it simply won't work—you'll only confuse her further and complicate your potty problems.

One or more of these factors may be the cause of your cat's litter box problems:

- **Litter box location and contents.** Some cats are particular about the type of litter they use, so if you've switched litter brands recently, try switching back to the old brand. If you've recently brought your kitty home from the pet store or shelter, try to find out what brand of litter they use and buy a bag of it.

  Cats also like to have their own litter box and may refuse to go in a box that's been used by another cat. And, as mentioned earlier, cats prefer to go in a clean place, so make sure you scoop out the waste from their box at least once a day, and wash the litter box once a week.

  Finally, make sure the litter box is in a location that your cat likes. Generally, cats don't want to do their business in a high-traffic area, or anywhere too close to where they eat.

At the same time, they want it to be close at hand—for example, on the same level of the house where they spend most of their time.

- **Stress.** Stress can be a major cause of bathroom problems in cats. Your cat's stress can come from several places: moving to a new home, a new pet in the house, changes within the family structure (a new family member, or an existing family member leaving home), or any unwanted changes to her routine. Reducing these sources of stress may improve your cat's litter box performance. If you can't reduce the stressors, try to come up with ways of decreasing their impact on your poor cat. For example, if the source of stress is a new puppy in the house, try to keep the puppy in a separate part of the house to give your cat a break.

- **General Confusion.** Your cat might simply be confused— maybe because of stress or changes to her environment. If this is the case, try keeping her in one room for a couple of days so that she learns where the litter box is. When she does use the litter box properly, encourage this good behavior by praising her and giving her a treat.

- **Medical Conditions.** If your cat produces very little urine when she goes, or meows in pain when you pick her up, it might mean that she has a medical condition.

  Possible medical conditions include (but aren't limited to): feline lower urinary tract disease, inflammatory bowel disease, diabetes mellitus, hyperthyroidism, kidney or liver disease, or colitis. Conditions such as feline lower urinary tract disease, arthritis, anal sac disease, and certain forms of colitis may cause your cat pain when urinating or defecating, resulting in her litter box issues.

If you suspect that your cat may be ill, take her to see the vet immediately.

How Your Relationship With Your Cat Affects Training

Cats' hearing apparatus is built to allow the human voice to easily go in one ear and out the other.

—STEPHEN BAKER, *How to Live with a Neurotic Cat*

While a lot of us treat our cats like children, the fact of the matter is, cats can behave a lot like children. They know what they can get away with (and so many owners let their cats get away with murder just because they're so darn cute), and even the sweetest cat will occasionally test the limits of your patience. For example, I know for a fact that my beloved Miki walks on the kitchen counters when I'm not around the house to watch her—and if I happen to catch her in the act, she'll scamper back onto the floor with a little grumbling meow, sometimes even before I have a chance to open my mouth to scold her!

If you're the boss of your house (or the "alpha cat", as I like to call it) and your cat knows it, it'll make training that much easier. On the other hand, if your cat is the top dog, so to speak, and knows that she can get away with anything, you're simply going to have a more difficult time getting her to do what you want her to do.

If there's someone else in the household who acts as the "alpha" figure and whom your cat responds well to, it's a good idea to get that person involved in the training as well. It'll prove very helpful if your kitty knows that all of the loving humans in her life want her to use the toilet.

Of course, all of this assumes that you're on good terms with your kitty. Toilet training is much less effective if you're a stranger to the cat, so if you aren't already friends with the cat you're trying to train, you need to make friends before you start. When I'm helping friends or family to train their cats, I always have the cat's loving guardian be the one to handle, coax and praise the cat.

Toilet training is much easier if the cat wants to please you, and a cat's not going to want to please you if it doesn't know and like you.

Teaching Your Cat Right From Wrong

Essentially, you do not so much teach your cat as bribe him.
—LYNN HOLLYN, author

Cats are pretty smart. They know when you're happy with them and when you're not. And while you probably won't be able to teach them to play chess or do your taxes for you, you *are* able to teach them the difference between good and bad behavior. You're doing this whenever you praise them for doing something good—like using a scratching post—or scold them for doing something bad—like scratching your couch. I'll bet you've probably been praising and scolding your cat naturally, whether you've been doing it consciously or not.

The technical term for this is *operant conditioning.* Operant conditioning, a term first coined in 1938 by psychologist B.F.

Skinner,[1] is a set of principles that describe how your cat (or any animal, in fact) learns to survive in her environment through reinforcement (consequences). With this type of learning, your cat's learned behaviors are dictated by the consequences that follow them. For example, if your cat goes on the toilet and you give her a treat, she'll be more likely to repeat the behavior. On the other hand, if your cat goes on the toilet and you squirt her with a water gun, she'll be less likely to repeat the behavior in the future. (Never squirt your cat with a water gun when she's on the toilet, by the way!)

There are four possible consequences to behavior within operant conditioning. They are:

1. Positive Reinforcement: Involves an addition of a good consequence when your cat does something you like. Your cat does her business in the toilet, so you give her praises and treats. This will increase the likelihood of the behavior occurring again.

2. Negative Reinforcement: Involves the removal of a bad consequence when your pet does something you like. For example, say your cat is accustomed to getting a much-hated bath after each time she trudges out onto the balcony and gets dirty. If, on the other hand, your cat comes inside and uses the toilet, you reward this behavior by skipping the bath. The absence of the expected bath reinforces the good behavior and serves to increase the likelihood of the behavior in the future. (We won't be using any negative rein-

---

[1] Skinner, B.F., *The Behavior of Organisms: An Experimental Analysis*, 1938. ISBN 1-58390-007-1, ISBN 0-87411-487-X.

forcement techniques for our kitty toilet training; I only mention it here because it's a key component of operant conditioning.)

3. Positive Punishment: Involves the presentation of a bad consequence when the behavior is performed. For instance, if your cat decides to poop in your bathtub, you bring her to the tub, show her the mess, and gently but firmly tell her "No". This decreases the likelihood of the behavior in the future. Other examples of positive punishment include:

   • Puppy urinates on the rug → puppy gets spanked with rolled-up newspaper.
   • Child hits his sister → child gets spanked by parents.
   • Man stays out late drinking with his friends → man gets spanked by wife (figuratively speaking).

4. Negative Punishment: Involves the removal of a good consequence when the behavior is performed. For example, you're praising your cat while she's prowling around the toilet seat, preparing to go, but in the end she elects not to go, so you stop all praise and put away the treat you were about to give her. The cat's refusal to go causes what she wants and likes (your praises and the promise of treats) to go away.

Our focus will be on positive reinforcement and negative punishment. On the positive reinforcement front, what I want you to do is practice **concentrated affirmation**. Concentrated affirmation means to supercharge the positive reinforcement by absolutely smothering your kitty with an inordinate amount of praise for doing something *really* good—but stop the praise completely after the good behavior stops. So, shower your cat with praise while she's on the toilet and while you're treating her afterwards, but praise her for no more than 15 seconds after she's finished her business. If you praise her too much for too long, the praise you give her while she's on the toilet won't be as meaningful to her, and she won't know exactly what she's being praised for.

Positive *punishment* will come into play if and when your cat has an accident. We'll discuss the proper way to reprimand your cat in the chapter "Correcting Accidents and Undesirable Behaviors". For now, just remember to praise your cat to no end whenever she's on the toilet!

When Should I Treat My Cat?

This might seem like an obvious question, but I actually get asked this a lot. The general rule of thumb is, praise your cat while she's going in the toilet, so she knows exactly what she's being praised for. Give her a treat as soon as she's done. The benefits of treating as soon as possible is twofold:

1. A cat will normally dig around the area after they've done their business in order to cover the scent of their waste. Your cat will start pawing the litter, the toilet seat, the toilet lid.... We want to train her to forget about covering up her scent, and get her to feel okay about leaving her waste untouched. So to do this, lure her away from the toilet with a treat, and while she's munching away on it, give the toilet a flush, so that when she comes back to investigate, her potty spot will be nice and clean.

2. We want to make sure that she associates the treat with go-
    ing #1 or #2 in the toilet. In an ideal world, we'd treat *while*
    she's going in the toilet, but, of course, this isn't really pos-
    sible... you don't want to interrupt her while she's going! So,
    we'll do the next best thing—treat immediately after she's
    finished her business. Remember to praise her all the while
    (for a maximum of 15 seconds).

Some cats are shy poopers, other cats couldn't care less
about privacy. If your cat won't use the bathroom while you're
around, it might be difficult to praise her while she's using the
bathroom. If this is your dilemma, you can employ a few stealth
maneuvers to catch her in the act.... Don't hang out in the bathroom, but keep an eye on your cat and take notice when she
saunters into the bathroom. Give her a few moments to settle in
(you'll get better at timing this once you get used to the sound of
litter rustling and kitty paws tromping around the toilet seat).
Once she's assumed the #1 or #2 position, she'll have committed
herself to going and won't stop for anything, at which point you
can walk into the bathroom and start praising her.

If your presence is deterring your cat from going to the bathroom, though, then don't do this every time—you don't want
your cat to associate the toilet with any negative feelings. It's
good enough to do this once in a while to let her know that her
guardian highly approves of her going in the human toilet. If
you aren't able to praise her while she's on the toilet every time,
just remember to always praise her immediately *after* she's done
as often as possible, and of course, make sure to give her a treat
each and every time.

Of course, it should also go without saying that you
shouldn't do anything to distract her while she's on the toilet,
especially if she's a shy pooper. Resist the temptation to open or

close the door, blow-dry your hair, or practice your new crash cymbals.... Give your cat the peace and quiet that anyone would want while relieving oneself!

❸

Training Yourself

As anyone who has ever been around a cat for any length
of time well knows, cats have enormous patience with
the limitations of the human mind.
—CLEVELAND AMORY, *The Cat Who Came for Christmas*

I had been told that the training procedure with cats was
difficult. It's not. Mine had me trained in two days.
—BILL DANA, comedian

Okay, so now you know that your cat can be trained. But can
you train *yourself?* Here are a few simple but vital things
that you'll need to remember when you train your cat.

Lid Up, Seat Down

After you use the toilet, remember: **keep the lid up, and the seat
down.** Having a toilet trained cat won't do you any good if the
toilet isn't available for your cat to use! If you think you or others in your household are going to forget, or even if you have

*Figure 3 Keep the toilet lid up and the seat down, and if neces-
sary, duct tape the lid so that it doesn't fall down. Also, leave a
sticky note on your toilet to remind yourself if you're prone to
forget*

guests over, write it down on a sticky note and stick it on the
toilet as a reminder.

If the lid of your toilet isn't very secure and is prone to falling shut, then you should either remove the lid entirely, or tape
it to the toilet tank so that it stays open. Duct tape is great for
this, since cats can't chew through it as easily as masking tape or
scotch tape.

Keep the Bathroom Door Open

If you're used to closing the bathroom door, remember to leave it open.

Some cats will come to you to complain if they really have to use the bathroom, but are unable to because the bathroom door is closed or the toilet seat is up. We really don't want it to get to that point—we want kitty to be able to go as she pleases, comfortably and stress-free. This is especially important while she's learning: if she's not used to using the toilet and can't access it anyway, she'll just pick the next best place to go, like in the bathtub or on the floor.

The 4 P's of Toilet Training

The final component of your training is the 4 P's of kitty toilet training: Preparation, Patience, Persistence, and Praise.

These might seem obvious, but it's easy to skim over these points and forget about them. You're already preparing yourself by reading this (and resisting the urge to jump ahead to the chapter on the toilet training procedure)... and good for you for doing this. But you should also be prepared that your cat will likely experience setbacks and accidents, and you'll need plenty of patience and persistence to stick with the training process.

Patience is key. Resist the urge to yell at your cat if she has an accident, and never, ever rub her nose in her mess. Trust me, I know how frustrating it can get when your cat lays a big poop on your favorite rug, but yelling and punishing her will do much more harm than good. Your cat won't know why you're being mean to her, and will likely just associate her bad feelings with *you* and not with anything she's done. As mentioned before, it's important that you have a positive relationship with your cat—if you do, you'll have much better success getting her to do what you want.

(If your cat has an accident, we're not going to let her get away with it scot-free, either; we'll go into techniques for reprimanding your cat in the chapter "Correcting Accidents and Undesirable Behaviors".)

Finally, remember to give your cat lots and lots of praise for a job well done. It might feel strange for you to do at first, and if your cat isn't used to all the attention, she might look at you like you're nuts... but trust me, it works wonders, and it'll all be worth it in the end!

Monitor Your Cat's Current Toilet Schedule

There's one final bit of homework for you before we get started, and that's to monitor your cat's bathroom cycles. If you aren't already familiar with your cat's usual potty schedule, you'll need to get acquainted with it. Does she like to go right after you've fed her? How many times a day does she go #1 and #2? How many hours is it between each trip to the bathroom?

This information will be useful to help you catch her in the act. You'll want to be present as much as possible to praise and treat your kitty. The more you're there to praise and treat her while she's on the toilet, the quicker the toilet training will go.

Knowing your cat's bathroom schedule will also be useful later on to detect bathroom avoidance behavior. It's almost a sure bet that your cat will show some signs of hesitation and use the bathroom less often than she used to, and we want to make sure that she doesn't hold it in for too much longer than she normally would. For example, say your cat usually defecates every 24 hours, but changes her schedule to go only once every 48 hours at some point during the toilet training. You'll know then that she's holding it in, and that you should slow your progress down a bit to give her more time to get comfortable with the current stage of training.

❹

Proper Diet and Nutrition

There is no snooze button on a cat who wants breakfast.
—ANONYMOUS

Okay, I know you're anxious to get started with the training and that you may be wondering: Why am I talking about diet and nutrition, and what does it have to do with training my cat? Well, as it turns out, this is probably the single biggest reason why so many toilet trainers fail: they don't take into account that their poor kitty is constipated!

Constipation is the enemy of toilet training. If your cat is constipated and her stools are hard as rocks, it'll be much harder for her to do #2 just in her litter box, never mind balancing over the human toilet. The harder it is for her to do her business, the more likely it is that she'll exhibit toilet avoidance behaviors. She may even start associating the pain and discomfort of her constipation with the toilet itself, and decide that it's just not a good place to go #2. Worse still, constipation may lead to further health problems if left unchecked over a period of time. So, it's in our best interest to prevent it before it starts.

The key to preventing constipation is to keep your cat's stool soft in the first place. If your cat's stool is hard, it causes constipation, which in turn causes toilet avoidance behaviors. Then the toilet avoidance causes the stool to get even harder. It's a vicious cycle.

This is where diet and nutrition come into play. Keeping your cat's stool soft is mainly a matter of proper hydration—we need to make sure your cat is consuming enough water. Many domestic cats don't get enough water in their diet, so we want to do everything we can to encourage them to drink more.

Change the Water Dish Daily

Cats prefer their water fresh, so encourage your cat to drink lots of it by cleaning her water dish and changing her water every day. Also try giving your cat multiple sources of water. Cats tend to drink more water if their water dish is *not* next to the food dish, so keep at least one source of water in a spot other than where she usually eats and drinks. (For instance, I put a cup of water on the bathtub ledge for my own cat—I figure she likes to lap up the water in the bathtub anyway, so why not give her a fresh cup to drink from?)

Pet Fountains

Cats also love running water, since it's fresh... and even if it's not, at least it appears that way to them. In nature, moving water is usually much fresher than a stagnant pool, since moving water draws oxygen from the air into the water. You may have noticed your own cat drinking from a dripping faucet, or even putting her paw in her water dish and swirling it around to simulate "running" water.

Figure 4 *Pet fountains simulate running water, which may encourage your cat to drink from it more often*

Pet fountains can achieve the same effect by keeping the water flowing, and they also filter the water to keep it pure. They're not cheap, but if you feel your cat's not drinking enough and really want to encourage her to drink more, it's well worth the cost. One person told me it was worth it just to keep her cat from jumping up onto the kitchen counters to drink from the sink!

Canned Wet Food

It's vital for cats to ingest water with their food, since they don't have very strong thirst drives.

In the wild, cats obtain most of their water from their prey, which contains approximately 70% to 75% water. Dry foods contain only 10% water, whereas canned wet foods contain approximately 78% water—providing a much better substitute for what your cat would normally consume in the wild. It's true that a cat on a dry food diet will naturally drink more water, but even if we take that into consideration, in the end a cat on dry food consumes approximately half the amount of water as a cat on wet food![4]

If your cat is on a dry food diet, make the switch to canned wet food now. Because wet foods contain significantly more water than the dry variety, you'll dramatically increase your cat's hydration level.

The Skinny on Wet Food versus Dry Food

Unfortunately, most of us don't put too much thought into what we feed to our pets. Worse still, there's quite a bit of misinformation out there about cat food. If you watch a lot of commercials for cat food, you might fall under the impression that dry food is healthier than the wet variety. Regrettably, this just isn't the case... not only that, it's detrimental to our toilet training. There's a wealth of information out there about feline nutrition in books, papers, and the Internet, but I'll just explain the basics here.

Water Content in Wet Foods

As mentioned previously, the water content in canned wet foods is much higher than that of dry foods. Wet foods do a much better job of hydrating cats, which is doubly important because they don't have very strong thirst drives in the first place.

---

[4] Lisa Pierson, DVM. "Feeding Your Cat: Know the Basics of Feline Nutrition." *CatInfo.org.*

Cats Are Carnivores

Cats are strict carnivores—they need to eat meat! It can be easy to forget that our feline friends are descendants of wild animals (although I know a few cat owners who would argue that their kitties are *still* extremely wild creatures!). Cats in the wild don't eat grains or other forms of carbohydrates, and neither should our domesticated kitties.

Cats have a requirement for dietary protein two to three times that of omnivores and herbivores.[5] While cats do have the ability to utilize carbohydrates in foods, their digestion and metabolism are more suited to high meat diets. For example, cats lack a sweet taste receptor, lack salivary amylase (enzyme to break down simple sugars), and have a lower activity of carbohydrate-specific digestive and metabolic enzymes.[6]

In the wild, your cat would be consuming a meat-based diet that's high in protein and moisture, with a moderate level of fat and less than 5% carbohydrate content, if any at all.

That's why it's a bit disheartening that most commercial cat food manufacturers load their dry foods with carbohydrates. They rely heavily on grains, cereals and vegetable products to manufacture their food, not because they hold any nutritional value, but because they don't require as much care and attention to preserve and maintain shelf life, which lowers the cost of the product. Car-

---

[5] Kim Russell, Peter R Murgatroyd, and Roger M Batt. "Adaptation of net protein oxidation to dietary protein intake in the domestic cat (Felis silvestris catus)." The Journal of Nutrition. 132:456-460, 2002.

[6] Debra L. Zoran. "The carnivore connection to nutrition in cats." *Vet Med Today: Timely Topics in Nutrition.* JAVMA, Vol 221, No. 11, December 1, 2002.

bohydrates can easily make up 40% of commercial dry foods.[7]

Is Dry Food Ever A Good Idea?

While there *are* good and nutritious brands of dry food out there that are made from quality ingredients, the same brand of wet food will invariably be better for your cat, simply for the hydration factor alone. The only real benefit of dry food is that it's more convenient for humans—it's cheaper for us to manufacture and less unpleasant for us to serve.

There is a widely held belief that dry foods help to clean teeth and remove tartar, improving your cat's dental health. If you think about it, though, it doesn't make much sense; would eating crackers improve *your* dental hygiene? Some cat food companies have actively promoted this idea, despite the fact that there's little scientific evidence to support it.

Still, a quality dry food is a way to provide your cat with nutrients at a lower cost than wet food—just make sure that at least **half** of your cat's diet is wet food. Also, if you do feed your cat dry food, just remember not to mix it with water, milk, or canned food in hopes of increasing her water intake. The reason for this is because dry food is exposed to bacteria during the final manufacturing process, even after the food is cooked and sterilized. When the food is exposed to moisture, the bacteria multiply rapidly. Some of those bacteria are dangerous and can make your cat sick, causing vomiting or diarrhea.

If In Doubt...

This is the approach to feline nutrition that I personally take, based on the research that I've conducted. The topic is somewhat

---

[7] Mordecai Siegal. *The Cornell Book of Cats: The Comprehensive and Authoritative Medical Reference for Every Cat and Kitten. 2nd Ed.* Villard, 1997.

controversial, and I'm sure the wet food versus dry food debate will continue for the foreseeable future. If you are in doubt, or if your cat is on a specific veterinarian-prescribed diet for health reasons, I highly encourage you to consult your veterinarian and to do your own research before making any changes your cat's diet. Check out the appendix at the end of this book for a list of resources to help you get started.

Choosing A Brand of Canned Wet Food

Cat owners are spoiled for choice when it comes to buying food for their pets. Unfortunately, that's not always a good thing. How do you choose a good brand that's healthy for your cat?

As with most things in life, you usually get what you pay for—higher quality brands are going to cost more than the $0.80 cans that you see at the supermarket. The key to choosing a good brand is to simply read the ingredient label on the side of the can. It won't depend so much on what's listed on the ingredient label, but what's *not* listed on the label. Try to avoid foods that contain fillers such as corn, wheat, soy, and gluten. Also, avoid any foods that contain animal digest or meat by-products, especially if it's listed as one of the first ingredients. Animal digest is basically the parts of animals that slaughterhouses can't sell to anyone else, so it's chemically treated and added to cat food. Meat by-product consists of anything not considered meat, and include parts typically not eaten by humans—intestines, lungs, and spleens. In the case of poultry by-products, it includes parts such as chicken heads, feet and beaks.

Figure 5 *Feeding your cat grain-free, high quality canned wet foods such as Wellness® or Nature's Variety® Instinct™ will benefit the health of your cat, and make toilet training much easier*

Two examples of quality brands that you can try are Nature's Variety® Instinct™ and the grain-free varieties of Wellness® (look for the yellow triangle on the label that indicates that it's grain-free). These are both popular brands that are well known for their quality, and are readily available at most pet supply stores. (And if you're accustomed to buying your cat food from a grocery store, you'll probably save a bit of money by not buying at inflated supermarket prices.)

A quality cat food may seem significantly more expensive, but your cat may actually eat less of it. The higher quality cat foods are free from by-products and starchy fillers, packing more nutrients and calories into a smaller serving, which benefits your cat's digestion and lowers her weight and amount of waste produced.

If these brands are a little too pricey for your liking, then the very least you should do is carefully read the labels and choose the best of the cheaper brands. Even the cheapest brand will have a few varieties, some of which may be better than others. For example, one of my friends serves inexpensive cans of Friskies to her cat, but she only buys the varieties that limit the aforementioned extraneous ingredients and don't have by-products as the primary component. Friskies' "Senior Sliced with Lamb and Rice" flavor lists meat by-product as its first ingredient and also contains corn, wheat gluten, and soy, whereas the "Whitefish and Tuna Dinner" has actual ocean whitefish as its first ingredient, and contains none of the unnecessary fillers. The choice is easy—get the Whitefish and Tuna Dinner.

Of course, if you want to go whole hog, you may want to look into feeding your cat what she would normally eat in the wild—raw meat. Some studies have shown that cats on a raw meat diet are healthier and more able to resist infection from disease-causing organisms. Be warned, however, that preparing a raw meat dinner from scratch can get messy and expensive, and care must be taken to ensure that the meat is clean and contaminant-free. Thankfully, you also have the option of going to a specialty pet store and choosing one of the many commercially available raw diets, which is a little pricier but much more convenient. It's also a good way to get important variety into your cat's raw meat diet.

If you're interested in learning more on the subject of feline nutrition, I recommend that you do some research to find a brand of cat food that you're comfortable serving to your own cat. There are some excellent resources online—check out the great ConsumerSearch.com article listed in the appendix at the end of this book, as well as the other resources that I've listed there.

Add Pumpkin to Your Cat's Diet

Canned pumpkin is very rich in fiber and is a good remedy for relieving the occasional bout of constipation. It's also good for diarrhea as well. (Note that I'm referring to canned pumpkin in its puréed form. Some pet stores also sell it in frozen packages.) If your cat is constipated, try adding one to two teaspoons of it to her regular meal—it will soften her stool, often in as little as a few hours.

Figure 6 Canned pumpkin

If constipation is a problem for your cat, we'll discuss solutions to this problem in greater detail in the "Warning Signs" chapter.

❺

Training Equipment

To do good work, one must first have good tools.
—CHINESE PROVERB

Experience is directly proportional to the amount of
equipment ruined.
—HARRISBERGER'S FOURTH LAW OF THE LAB

Toilet training your cat requires some training equipment.
Here's what you'll need.

Roasting Pan

The roasting pan is going to be our tool of choice for toilet training. I'm referring to the disposable pans that are made of aluminum—they're readily available at any grocery store for around
two dollars. Sizes vary slightly between manufacturers, but you
should be able to find one that measures around 11¾" × 9¼" ×
2½". A roasting pan this size will fit snuggly inside your toilet
bowl.

Figure 7 *A brand new roasting pan*

The roasting pan will serve as your cat's litter box for the next little while. (We'll get into the details on installing the pan in your toilet bowl and how to use it in the next chapter, "The Toilet Training Process".)

Flushable Litter

If you aren't already using a brand of litter that's flushable, I highly recommend that you switch to one before you start toilet training. During the toilet training process, your cat will un-avoidably paw a bit of litter into the toilet—and you don't want to have too much non-flushable litter end up down there. It will also be extremely convenient for you to be able to flush everything away, instead of having to scoop and throw the waste in the trash.

So, before you start toilet training, dump the old litter from her litter box, replace it with the flushable kind, and allow her a day or two to get comfortable with the new litter in her litter box. Some cats will take to a new brand of litter without any complaints, but others may balk at the change. If your cat resists, what you can do is mix a bit of the new litter with the old stuff at first, and then gradually increase the amount of new litter until her litter box contains 100% of the flushable stuff.

There are many brands of flushable litter out there, and most will work for our toilet training purposes. Personally, I recommend World's Best Cat Litter™ or Swheat Scoop®. Recycled paper litter is fine as well—the small amounts that fall into the toilet shouldn't pose any problems. Try to avoid flushable crystal litter, as they make a sizzling noise when exposed to water. When your cat inevitably paws some of it into the toilet, the sizzling noise may distract or frighten her, making the training a more daunting experience.

During the training process, remember to change the litter frequently. If your cat is like most cats, she's very likely a neat freak, so clean litter will help encourage her to use the toilet training set-up.

Padded / Wooden Toilet Seat

If you don't have a padded or wooden toilet seat, I highly recommend that you switch to one. Cats in general have an excellent sense of balance, but if you have a sloped plastic seat, it may be just too narrow and slippery. Make the switch to a padded seat or a wide wooden seat (oak, birch, maple, etc., and the wider the better).

Figure 8 A padded toilet seat is soft and plush, and provides good
grip to help your cat balance over the toilet

Also, make sure that the toilet seat is securely fastened to the
toilet bowl. If it's loose and slides around when your cat's
tromping around on it, she won't feel secure enough to use it.
We want to do everything we can to make it easier for kitty to
use the toilet!

If you've already started the toilet training and realize you
need to switch to a new toilet seat *after* you've begun, you
should gradually introduce her to the new seat. Put it down on
the floor of her favorite playroom for a day or two, and sprinkle
it with catnip to generate interest. When she rubs herself on the
new seat (or any object, including you), she'll transfer her scent
onto it with the scent glands in her cheeks, chins, and paws.

Once she's marked the new seat with her scent, install it on the toilet when she's not around to watch. (And don't forget: lid up, seat down!)

❻

The Toilet Training Process

It is better to take many small steps in the right direction than to make a great leap forward only to stumble backward.
—CHINESE PROVERB

Finally we get to the fun part—the kitty toilet training process itself! You've carefully read the previous chapters to prepare yourself for the training process. You've also made the required adjustments to your cat's diet, and you've acquired the training equipment that you'll need to do the training. If you haven't done these things, go back and do them... I'm serious! Make sure that you've prepared yourself and your cat for training; you won't be very successful otherwise.

Transitioning Your Cat to the Toilet

The basic concept behind toilet training your cat is to get your cat accustomed to seeing the toilet as an appropriate place to go potty. Our objective, of course, is to transition her from digging and pooping into a box of sand to doing her business into a big bowl of water. Piece of cake, right?

This seemingly insurmountable task isn't so daunting if we chip away at it bit by bit. The key is to split up the process into several stages in order to make the transition as easy as possible for both you and your cat. At each stage, the cat will learn a little something new, but we'll keep the changes in each stage to a minimum to keep things manageable for her. We'll also provide "bridges" between each stage whenever necessary—cues that the cat can understand to help her move from one stage to the next. And of course, we'll move slowly with the training and only go as fast as our kitty is comfortable with.

The 5 Stages of Toilet Training

Our transition from litter box to toilet consists of 5 stages. In each stage, we'll make a small change to the potty set-up, give your cat time to adjust, and then make another small change. And if at any time your cat gets frustrated, confused, or just decides that the whole thing isn't worth it and poops in the bathtub, it's a sure sign that you're pushing her too fast; back up a stage or two to give her more time to get used to it before proceeding any further.

Before embarking on a new stage, make sure that your cat has done #1 and #2 at least once. Also, each time you're ready to advance to the next stage, it's best to do it immediately after your cat does #2—this will allow your cat to start the next stage with a #1. It makes it a bit simpler for them to get comfortable with the change, since it's easier for cats to squat for #1 than it is to squat for #2.

Stage 1: Litter Box Beside the Toilet

The purpose of this stage is to get your cat accustomed to hopping up onto the toilet to do her business. This will be the easiest stage of the training, and most cats can blow through this fairly quickly. (In fact, if your cat is young or you know that she's easygoing and adaptable, you can try skipping this stage altogether and move on to Stage 2, although following through with this stage will definitely help ease your cat into the next one.)

Start by moving the cat's litter box from wherever it is to the side of the toilet. Make sure she knows where it is—if necessary, pick her up and put her in the box to show her the new location. Your cat should pick this up fairly quickly; cats determine an appropriate place to go potty largely based on smell and where they've gone before, so as long as they can detect the familiar smell of their litter, they should have no problem with the new litter box location.

(Conversely, if your cat ever has an accident on the floor, rug, carpet, etc., it's imperative that you clean the area properly; otherwise, she might think it's appropriate to go there again, since she's marked it once before! Later, we'll discuss this in greater detail, as well as provide tips on how to remove the 'mark', in the chapter "Correcting Accidents and Undesirable Behaviors".)

Now that your cat has gone at least once in the new litter box location, it's time to gradually raise the box until it's level with the top of the toilet seat. Find something sturdy—for example, a cardboard box, or a stack of newspapers—and raise the litter box a couple of inches. (Don't use magazines or anything that's too slick, otherwise the litter box will slide around, making kitty feel insecure.) Wait a day or two for your cat to do #1 and #2 in the

Figure 9 Use cardboard boxes or newspapers to raise the litter box beside the toilet

Figure 10 Moving the litter box directly over the toilet

raised litter box, and once you're certain that she's gotten the hang of it, raise the box another couple of inches. Keep doing this until the litter box is level with the toilet seat.

Somewhere along this process, your cat will learn to jump up onto the toilet seat first and then step into the litter box from there. Of course, you've trained yourself to keep the toilet seat down and the lid up like we've discussed, so kitty is getting accustomed to navigating around on the open toilet seat.

Once the litter box is level with the top of the toilet seat, move the litter box over so that it's sitting directly over the seat. If you've noticed that your cat has been hesitant to make the previous changes, you may want to move the litter box over the toilet seat gradually—move it halfway onto the seat at first, then fully over the seat. Also, make sure that the litter box is secure—we don't want the litter box to move around and potentially fall over! If necessary, use some duct tape to tape it down to the toilet.

At this point, feel free to get rid of the cardboard boxes or newspapers that you used to raise the litter box—we won't need them anymore.

Stage 2: Transitioning to the Litter Pan

Here comes the exciting part—we're going to get rid of the litter box entirely!

For this step, you'll need that roasting pan that we discussed in the previous chapter. This disposable pan is going to be where kitty does her business for the next little while.

Lift the toilet seat and put the pan inside—you might have to apply a bit of force to get it in, and the bottom corners of the pan will likely be crushed inwards a little bit. This is fine—we want the pan to be nice and snug inside the toilet, so when kitty

Figure 11 *The roasting pan sits securely inside the toilet bowl*

tromps around in her new litter pan, she'll feel nice and secure. The lip of the roasting pan should be resting more or less over the rim of the toilet bowl (although not completely, of course... we are trying to put a rectangular object into a round hole).

Now put down the toilet seat. Because the roasting pan is now between the seat and the toilet bowl, the seat probably won't sit as flush (no pun intended) with the bowl as it normally would. To remedy this, just apply a little gentle pressure on the seat to help flatten out any irregular bumps in the roasting pan and secure our setup.

Some toilet seats have hinges that protrude out, which might interfere with the roasting pan. If your toilet seat's hinges are preventing you from putting down the seat properly, you can cut

Figure 12 *Miki uses the toilet with a roasting pan full of litter. The roasting pan sits snuggly in the toilet bowl (underneath the toilet seat).*

notches in the roasting pan to give the hinges space to move up and down.

Bridging the transition from litter box to roasting pan

Before getting your cat to use the roasting pan for the first time, do a wholesale change of the litter in her litter box, so that she gets to use her litter box one last time with fresh, clean litter.

Once she's gone #1 and #2 once more in the litter box, it's time to make the transition to the roasting pan. Clean out any clumps from the litter box, and fill the roasting pan with the used litter. It might be a little bit unpleasant for you to handle used litter, but at least it's only been used once, so it's relatively clean. The smell of the used litter will provide a familiar signal to her that this is where she's supposed to go, and will help bridge the gap between litter box and litter pan. Don't overdo it with the litter—an inch of it should suffice.

With any luck, your cat will be using the roasting pan as her new litter box without fuss. Make sure you hide away her old litter box in a place where she can't find it—we don't want the presence or even the smell of the old litter box to confuse her during this stage.

Stage 3: Introducing the Water

This is the stage that's usually the trickiest for most cats— introducing kitty to the water in the toilet bowl. If your cat is anything like the majority of cats, then water is probably not her friend. (Many cats *do* enjoy water, and some will want to play with the water in the toilet or even drink out of it... and if your cat is one of them, we'll discuss solutions to this problem in the chapter "Correcting Accidents and Undesirable Behaviors".)

Because this step will likely be one of the toughest ones for your cat, try to do this on a Friday night (assuming that you don't work weekends), because you'll want to be around for the next couple of days to monitor her reaction.

For this stage, take out the roasting pan from the toilet, re- move the litter that's in it, and get out a pair of scissors. The key here is to introduce the water very, very slowly by cutting the smallest of holes in the pan. Later, we'll gradually enlarge the hole, but for now, we want it to be small enough so that your cat doesn't get spooked by Niagara Falls rushing beneath her.

The size of the hole that you should start with will depend on how well your cat's doing. If your cat's been handling all of

Figure 13 *Roasting pan with 1" × 1" hole cut in the corner. The excess flap is folded up to create a litter dam.*

the changes so far without batting an eyelash and is using the toilet according to her usual schedule, then you can start with a relatively large hole—1" × 1" or even bigger. On the other hand, if your cat has shown reluctance to previous changes, you may want to start off with a pencil-sized hole, so that she might not even notice it at first. Slowly enlarge that pencil-sized hole to a 1" × 1" hole as your cat gets more comfortable with it.

If you're starting with a 1" × 1" hole or larger, make sure you don't cut away the excess aluminum; instead, cut the roasting pan so that you can bend the excess aluminum up like a flap. The flap will serve as our litter "dam" to help block the litter from being pushed into the toilet by your cat. It won't prevent all of the litter from ending up in the toilet, but it'll help. This is important, especially as we enlarge the hole, because without the litter dam, your cat might paw all of the litter into the toilet before she's even ready to go—and then refuse to go because there's no litter left!

Where should the hole go?

Start the hole at one end of the toilet. Don't cut the hole right in the middle of the pan, otherwise we won't be able create the litter dam without seriously complicating our litter box contraption. Plus, it'll be easier for your cat to adjust to the hole if it's not smack dab in the middle of her pooping grounds... never mind the fact that there's a big scary pool of water right below!

Start the hole in the front of the pan, or in the back?

As you enlarge the hole in the roasting pan, your cat will automatically aim for the litter portion of the pan, and try her best to avoid going into the hole. As the area of litter gets smaller and smaller, she'll have less room for her paws, and so will be forced to learn how to put her paws on the toilet seat. She'll start by putting one of her front paws on the seat, then both front paws; then, as the litter pan gets too small for her hind legs, she'll put one hind leg on the seat, then finally, all four paws on the seat. The upshot of this is, if you start the hole at the front of the pan (towards the front of the toilet), your cat will gradually be pushed towards the back of the toilet as you enlarge the hole— she'll naturally position herself this way to make sure her poops land in the litter. When the hole gets small enough, she'll put her front paws on the back of the toilet seat, doing her business facing the toilet tank.

Conversely, if you start with the hole at the back of the toilet, the opposite will occur: she'll be forced to inch towards the front

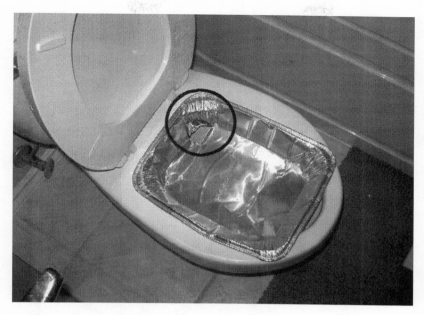

Figure 14 Roasting pan in the toilet, with the hole started at the back of the toilet

of the toilet as the hole gets bigger, thereby learning to face forward when the training process is over.

Our goal is to have kitty face the front of the toilet—so start with the hole at the back of the toilet. Here's why:

- **Freedom of paw placement.** If your cat faces forward, she'll have more space to experiment with paw positioning. On the other hand, if she faces the back of the toilet, the seat lid and toilet tank would be right in her face and get in her way, restricting her options for paw placement.

- **Splash-back.** Splash-back is detrimental to toilet training. Splash-back occurs when a #2 falls into the toilet and hits

Figure 15 *The water towards the front of the toilet is more shallow than the back. Training your cat to defecate into the front of the toilet will help to minimize splash-back*

the water with a splash, causing the unfortunate pooper's bum to get wet. Humans don't like splash-back, and it's a good bet that cats don't like it much either.

If we teach our cats to poop facing the front of the toilet, their stools will land in the shallow end of the toilet bowl, minimizing the amount of splash-back on their bums. (Take a look inside your toilet—you'll notice the depth of the water in the front of the bowl is shallower than in the back.) This is the primary reason for teaching cats to use the toilet facing forward instead of backward: if they're splashed with water every time they go #2, it won't be long before they find a less traumatic place to do their business!

Another Solution to Splash-Back

Getting your cat to poop in the shallow end of the bowl is a great way to minimize splash-back, but it might not get rid of it entirely. If you're still noticing some splash-back, a simple temporary solution is to put toilet paper in the toilet. Line the toilet paper as neatly as possible over the water, so that when your cat's poop falls into the toilet, the TP will cushion the fall. It's not really practical to do this over the long term, but it's good to do this while training to limit the variables that may be impeding your cat's progress.

Teaching a cat to face the back of the toilet isn't without its merits, however. The nice thing about it is that it introduces the cat to the water more gradually by exposing the shallow end of the toilet bowl first. In fact, depending on the shape of your particular toilet, if you cut the first hole in the front of the pan, you probably won't even expose any water at all. Give this method a try if your cat is extremely adverse to water, or if she's been slow to catch on to the toilet training changes thus far, or if she's just reluctant to go with the hole in the back of her litter pan.

Bridging the transition to exposed water

The key transitional block here, of course, is the water. If your cat has problems using the litter pan with all that scary water exposed, then get her used to the idea of having a hole in her litter pan first, without water, by starting with a small hole at the front of the pan. When kitty hops into the roasting pan and starts digging, she'll be able to see the litter that falls into the hole, lying in the shallow part of the toilet bowl. And when she sticks her face and paws inside the hole to investigate this strange hole, she'll get used to the presence of water, but she won't get her paws too damp, if at all.

Enlarge the hole to reveal the water only when you're certain that kitty is completely comfortable with the existing setup. When the hole is big enough and she's used to seeing the water, you can turn the roasting pan around so that the hole is at the back of the toilet. It shouldn't be too confusing for your cat; she'll follow where the litter goes, and figure out how to reposition herself to face the front of the toilet.

Tricking your cat into accepting the hole in the roasting pan

If your cat absolutely refuses to use the toilet with even the tiniest hole in the roasting pan, here's a last-resort technique that you can use to trick your cat into doing it.

First, observe where your cat is sitting in the roasting pan. Odds are, she usually sits in the same area every time: either leaning to the right or the left, facing the front or the back. Whatever the case, there will be a part of the pan that's exposed and accessible to you while she's doing her business. Make a note of where this spot is, then take out the pan and make your 1" × 1" hole in that spot.

What we're going to do is make a trap door that we can push open while kitty is squatting over the toilet. When she prepares to go, it will appear to her that she has a full pan of litter; once she commits herself to the squatting position and starts going, you'll poke the trap door open with a stick, revealing the water below.

To make the trap door, cover the hole with a small piece of cardboard (just a little bigger than the 1" × 1" hole) on the underside of the pan. Use a piece of duct tape to tape the cardboard down. Just make sure that you don't use too much tape on one end of the cardboard—if it sticks too hard, you won't be able to poke it open very easily. You don't want to have to apply too much force to get the trap door open, lest you scare your cat while she's on the toilet.

Now put the roasting pan back into the toilet (making sure it's oriented correctly so that the trap door is in the right spot) and fill it with litter. Observe your cat the next few times she uses the set-up; once she's committed to the squatting position and is going #1 or #2, poke the trap door open. When your cat finishes her business, she'll inspect the set-up, notice the hole and the water below, and finally realize that the whole thing's not so bad after all.

Stage 4: Enlarging the Hole and Teaching Proper Paw Position

Okay, so now your cat's gotten used to that 1" × 1" hole you cut in the roasting pan. Now let's turn that 1" × 1" hole into a 1" × 2" hole—get out your pair of scissors, and expand the hole lengthwise (i.e. along the short side of the roasting pan). Remember to fold the excess aluminum flap so that it creates a dam to block litter from falling into the hole.

Keep expanding the hole like this until eventually the hole becomes a rectangular strip right across the roasting pan. Once we have this rectangular hole, enlarging it will simply be a matter of making a small cut into both sides of it and rolling up the aluminum flaps like a sardine can.

During the next few bathroom cycles, keep enlarging the hole a little bit each time kitty goes #1 and #2 successfully, and keep cutting down or folding over the excess aluminum to maintain the litter dam at a reasonable height. Also, make sure you leave

Figure 16 *Roasting pan with the 1" × 1" hole enlarged to 1" × 2"*

Figure 17 *Roasting pan with the hole enlarged all the way across*

just under an inch of litter in the pan at all times. And remember, if at any time kitty seems nervous enough to start doing her business on your bathroom mat, just leave the setup alone for a few days to give her time to get used to it.

If your cat is a digger (and odds are she is), litter is probably winding up in the toilet. That's fine, since you're using flushable litter, right? If she paws too much litter into the toilet, just remember to add more litter to the roasting pan. Try to maintain it so that the litter is just under an inch high at all times.

At some point, the hole will get large enough so that your cat's waste lands in the water in the toilet bowl instead of in the litter. Praise your kitty like crazy... this is a big moment for her! Doing #1 and #2 into the water will seem strange for your cat at first, but once she realizes that the water is a "magic litter" that does a better job of neutralizing the odor than her regular litter, she likely won't mind it one bit.

Reinforcing the Roasting Pan

As the hole in the roasting pan gets larger, the structural integrity of the pan might weaken, making your cat feel more precarious about sitting in the thing.

If the roasting pan doesn't seem sturdy enough to support your cat—for example, if you notice that the pan wobbles under the weight of your cat, or the litter dam keeps getting pushed down by your cat's pawing—try the handyman's universal solution to all repair problems: duct tape!

A couple of layers of duct tape wrapped around the bottom and sides of the roasting pan will help strengthen it, which will provide extra support for your cat's weight and allow her to feel more secure about using it.

Also, if the litter dam is unable to withstand your cat's digging and keeps getting knocked down, wrapping duct tape around the sides of the dam will help to fortify it and keep it propped up.

Keep on enlarging the hole until there's nothing left of the roasting pan except a 1" strip of litter. In the next stage, we'll work on eliminating this last bit of litter completely. At this point, your cat will have at least three paws on the toilet seat, if not all four.

Figure 18 Hole in the roasting pan has been cut back to the point where only a 1" strip of litter remains

Teaching Proper Paw Position

Our final goal is to have your cat squat with all four of her paws on the toilet seat, but this won't happen immediately.

Before you cut the hole in the roasting pan, your cat probably started with all four of her paws in the litter pan whenever she went to the bathroom.

As the hole grows and the amount of litter decreases, your cat will do her best to aim for the litter, and will naturally find comfortable squatting positions to make this possible. When the hole gets big enough, she'll start going with her front paws on the toilet seat, hind legs in the litter. Eventually, when the roasting pan gets small enough, she'll learn to put one of her hind paws on the toilet seat. And when the roasting pan gets so small that she can't put any of her paws in it, she'll finally learn to put all four paws on the toilet seat.

Most cats will learn this naturally, but some cats that are a bit slower (but no less special, of course) might need some help with that last leg. If you notice that the roasting pan is getting too small for your cat's last hind leg, but she's still desperately hanging on the last bit of the pan, try repositioning her paw for her—wait until she's committed to going, then pick up her paw and move it onto the toilet seat... and remember to praise her like crazy! She won't like being touched when she's going to the bathroom, but if you keep praising her and reward her with treats afterwards, she'll forgive you for this minor transgression. More importantly, she'll learn to get comfortable with the proper potty stance.

If you decide to try this, wait until your cat has learned to put three paws on the toilet seat first. We want to interfere as little as possible at the beginning of training.

Figure 19 *Miki demonstrates the proper paw position for doing*
#1

Stage 5: Eliminating the Litter

With Stage 4 complete, there's nothing left of the roasting pan except a 1" strip of litter. Your kitty is willingly doing her business straight into the water, and she has three if not all four paws on the toilet seat. Give yourself a pat on the back—you and your cat are almost at the finish line!

That last bit of litter might be something of a crutch for your cat. Some cats will do just fine if you take it away; other cats are completely addicted to litter and will refuse to go if it's not there. We won't take any chances at this stage, so play it safe and wean your cat off the litter gradually.

To do this, first remove a tiny bit of litter from the pan—shave about a millimeter off the top. (Actually, odds are your cat will do the work for you by pawing some litter into the toilet during the course of her digging, naturally reducing the litter in the pan. You might even need to add more litter if she paws too much into the toilet.)

Wait for her to go #1 and #2 again. Once she's used to having less litter in her pan, repeat the process, removing a little more litter from the pan. Keep doing this until there's no more litter in the pan.

Voilà! Your cat has now been weaned off her litter. Now all we have to do is wean her off of the roasting pan.

The Instinct to Dig

Your cat's probably started pawing or "digging" around the toilet seat, and maybe even the toilet lid, before and after she goes to the bathroom. This is perfectly normal—she's just satisfying her urge to cover up her waste in order to hide the smell from predators. Some cats let up on the digging after they've been toilet trained, once they realize that the water does just as good a job at covering up their scent and they relax a bit. For other cats, the digging instinct is so ingrained that they never give it up. Either way, don't worry too much about it; as sad as it might look to you, it isn't causing them any psychological damage. Even cats who aren't toilet trained do this—I've known more than a few litter box-using cats who pointlessly scratch around the floor outside of their litter box after going to the bathroom, even though there's no litter to dig at. It's just an innate habit that domestic cats inherited from their wild ancestors and never gave up.

Removing the Roasting Pan

If you're lucky, your cat is now using the toilet with all four paws on the toilet seat. If you're not, she's still got one hind leg resting on what's left of the roasting pan, using it as a ledge.

If you're one of the unlucky ones, not to worry—it just means we need to keep enlarging the hole, albeit at a slower pace. Get out your pair of scissors and cut away the litter dam (we don't need it anymore anyway, since there's no litter left in the pan that we need to prevent from falling into the toilet). This will make the ledge a little less stable, discourage her from using it, and persuade her to put that last leg on the seat.

If she still insists on putting one leg on the ledge, then gradually cut it away lengthwise an inch at a time. If you have a 1" × 9" strip left, cut it down to a 1" × 8" ledge, wait for your cat to do her business, then cut away another inch. Eventually, there won't be enough of the roasting pan for her to use as a ledge, and she'll be forced to teach herself to put all four paws on the toilet seat. Once she has all four paws on the toilet seat, the rest of the way is easy.

At this point, even though your cat isn't touching the roasting pan anymore when she uses the toilet, it might still be a psychological crutch. This is because she's gotten used to targeting the roasting pan, instead of aiming for the water. You can tell if

Figure 20 *Gradually cut away the 1" strip (the "ledge" of the roasting pan) inch by inch until your cat decides that putting her last leg on the seat is preferable to using the ledge. In this photo, approximately 3 inches of the ledge have been removed.*

this is the case with your cat if she's sniffing at the space between the toilet seat and the toilet bowl, inspecting it to ensure that the roasting pan is still there. You can try removing the roasting pan completely, but if your cat balks and refuses to use the toilet with the pan removed, you'll have to gradually wean her off it.

To do this, cut away any remnants of the roasting pan bottom an inch at a time. Then, gradually trim away the sides of the roasting pan until you can't see it at all when you look down inside the toilet bowl.

Stick with this set-up for a little while. Eventually, your cat will start targeting the water instead of the no-longer-visible roasting pan. After a few days, remove the pan entirely (but store it in a hidden place in case you need to backtrack).

Congratulations—**your cat is now toilet trained!**

Keep Monitoring Your Cat

For the next little while, keep an eye on your cat to make sure that she doesn't regress... even though she's successfully used the toilet once or twice, doesn't mean that she's not still wondering if it's easier to just go on the floor. If a cat is going to rebel against the toilet training, she'll usually do it after the first few days, so be vigilant about giving her treats and praise for the next week.

Once she's used the toilet by herself without incident for a week or more, consider your cat completely toilet trained!

Bonus Stage: Teaching Your Cat to Flush

You and your cat have come a long way, and if you wanted to stop at this point, I wouldn't blame you... your cat is already head and shoulders above the pack, and you have lots to be proud of!

If you're feeling inspired, though, here's how to conquer that last and most complex steps of kitty toilet training—getting your cat to flush the toilet. Be forewarned, though, that once your cat learns how to flush, you might not be able to control *when* they flush. Many cats who know how to flush tend to do it a *lot*—they just like to watch the water going down the toilet, and if they realize that they have the ability to initiate the "swirly water show" whenever they want, you might not like what it does to your water bill!

The Appeal of the "Swirly Water Show"

I didn't bother training my Miki to flush the toilet until she was about five years old. This was about the time when she finally got bored of watching the water swirl down the toilet bowl. Up until then, whenever I'd flush the toilet, she'd run up to it, reach up to put her two front paws on the seat, and stick her nose in the bowl to enjoy the show. I had read anecdotes of cats who liked to flush all day, and that was enough to deter me from teaching this skill to Miki until she had matured a little bit!

Even though Miki knows how to flush, she never caught on that she should do it right after she goes #1 or #2; usually, she'll only do it if I'm there to coax and encourage her. On the rare occasion, she'll flush when the mood strikes her—I can only surmise that she wants to clean her bowl, and that she's tired of waiting for a human to do it for her. I try not to question it too much; I'm just grateful to have a cat that doesn't flush incessantly whenever she's in need of entertainment.

If you want to witness what can happen when a more excitable cat learns how to flush the toilet, search YouTube or Google for Gizmo the toilet-flushing cat—there's a great video of this cat continually flushing the toilet for almost three minutes. No, he's not toilet trained—he just likes to watch the water swirl down the toilet, much to the annoyance of his owners.

Training a cat to flush can be a long and often tedious process, and it requires you to be home a lot to supervise your cat (the more often you can be with your cat while she uses the toilet, the faster the training will go). Unfortunately, there's also no guarantee of success... some cats can do it, and some cats just can't.

Of course, there are obvious benefits to having a cat that can flush. Coming home to a clean toilet is infinitely better than coming home to a bunch of poops floating in your toilet. And if you ever have any guests visiting your house and they use your bathroom at an inopportune time, they might start questioning your hygiene as well as your diet.

There are two methods of teaching a cat to flush that you can try: the Ball and String method, and the Handle Extension method. Each has its own set of pros and cons.

The Ball and String Method

The Ball and String method is the easier of the two methods for getting your cat to flush. The drawback to this method is that it's extremely difficult to condition your cat to flush only after she uses the toilet. It also requires that your cat is attracted to a ball tied to a piece of string, which some cats aren't, unless there's a human at the other end of the string swinging the ball around.

With the Ball and String method, you simply tie a toy ball (or her favorite plush toy) to a piece of string, and attach the other end of the string to the toilet handle. The ball should be dangling about a foot or two off of the ground. When your cat plays with the dangling ball, she'll grab on to it, pull the handle and flush the toilet. Eventually, she'll catch on that playing with the dangling ball causes the toilet to clean itself (and also initiates the "swirly water show").

After she's proven that she can flush the toilet, keep shortening the string length so that she's forced to jump higher for the ball. Eventually, the string will be so short that the ball touches

Figure 21 Use string to tie a ball or a toy to the toilet handle.
When your cat grabs on to the ball and pulls, the toilet will flush

Figure 22 Keep shortening the string until the ball touches the
toilet handle

the toilet handle. More often than not, she'll be pushing the handle itself.

While this method provides a nice and relatively easy way of getting your cat to flush, the problem, as mentioned previously, is that your cat doesn't learn *when* it's an appropriate time to flush. Some extremely clever cats are able to make the connection that, in order to clean their bathroom area, they should flush the toilet... and driven by instinct to cover up their waste, that's exactly what they'll do. For most cats, though, we can't expect their little kitty brains to make that connection all on their own.

To teach your cat to flush immediately after she goes to the bathroom, here's what you can do: once your cat is able to flush (with the ball on a short string, ball touching the handle), take the ball and string away until she uses the toilet. Whenever you catch her using the toilet, tie the ball and string on the handle while she's busy doing her business. Hopefully, she'll turn her attention to the ball right after she's done, swat the ball and flush the toilet. If she flushes successfully, make sure to give her a treat and praise her like crazy to help condition her to flush the next time she finishes using the toilet.

The Handle Extension Method

The Handle Extension method is harder to teach to your cat, but the benefit is that it provides a less enticing way of flushing the toilet than the Ball and String method. This will hopefully encourage your cat to only flush when she has to, and not whenever she feels like playing.

As the name suggests, the Handle Extension method involves extending the toilet handle. Toilet handles aren't designed for kitties, and most cats don't have enough strength to use them.

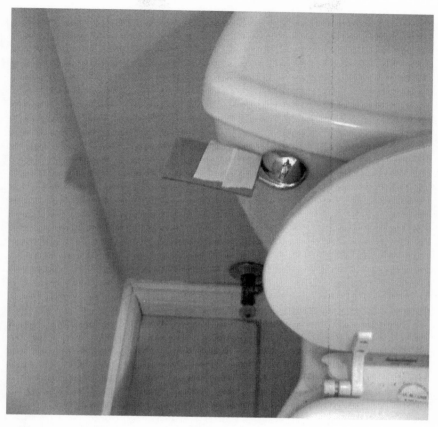

Figure 23 *Extend the toilet handle with a piece of cardboard to give your cat more leverage to push it down*

The solution to this is to extend the handle and make it longer, providing the cat with more leverage to push it down.

Building an extension for your toilet is going to take a little bit of ingenuity. For the extension, find a thick cardboard box and cut out a rectangular piece approximately 1.5" × 3". You can also use a piece of scrap plastic or metal that you might have lying around in your garage (just make sure there aren't any jagged edges, of course). Put the extension on the floor, sprinkle it with catnip and let your cat go nuts all over it (just like when you put catnip over her new toilet seat)—this will allow her to mark it with her scent and help her generate a positive association with it. After she's finished rubbing herself on it, tape it to the toilet handle. Give the end of the extension a push to test that it's strong and secure enough to actually flush the toilet. (If it's not, try cutting out another piece of cardboard and layer it on top of the original one to make the extension stronger.)

Now call your kitty over to the toilet—lure her to you with a treat, but put the treat away when she comes. Now that you've got her attention, take her two front paws into your hands, direct them over to the new handle extension, and push against it to flush. Now treat her. Repeat this process a few more times, treating each time the toilet flushes (but don't treat if the toilet doesn't actually flush). With any luck, your cat will catch on that flushing the toilet results in a reward. Keep doing this for the next few days until she's able to flush the toilet by herself.

Once your cat is able to flush, it's time to teach her when she should actually do it. The next time your cat finishes going #1 or #2, get a treat out and hold it over the handle to entice her to flush. If she flushes successfully, give her the treat; if not, put the treat away. From this point on, treat your cat only after she goes to the bathroom *and* successfully flushes.

It can be a very lengthy process, but with enough repetition and a bit of luck, you'll have conditioned your cat to flush after she uses the toilet.

If Neither Method Works For You...

Some cats just can't seem to get the hang of flushing the toilet, so don't feel too bad if your kitty can't manage it. If you're steadfast in your desire for a clean toilet bowl after every use, consider an automatic flusher. Many companies sell these for regular home toilets, and they do a very good job of detecting cats as well as humans. Just don't install it until well after your cat has mastered toilet training—you don't want the toilet to flush incessantly and distract your cat while she's trying to learn!

❼

Training With Multiple Cats

One cat just leads to another.
—ERNEST HEMINGWAY, American writer and journalist

If you have more than one cat in your household, toilet training will definitely be more complicated than training just one cat. It *can* be done, though, whether you're training two or more cats at the same time, or you already have a trained cat and you're introducing a new kitty into the household that you'd like to train.

Training More Than One Cat at the Same Time

The main obstacle to training multiple cats at the same time will be keeping track of who's doing what: if you discover an accident, it can be hard to figure out which cat to reprimand. Not only that, but some cats might not like sharing a toilet with another cat, especially if it's unflushed and dirty—just like how some cats dislike sharing soiled litter boxes with their four-legged housemates. It adds just one more reason why a cat may be refusing to use the toilet set-up.

For this reason, it's best to have one toilet for each cat that you're training, so that they don't have to share. But, if you don't have enough toilets to go around, don't fret about it too much; sharing a toilet is less stressful for cats than sharing a litter box, since the toilet won't smell like other cats quite as badly as a shared litter box would. If you have no choice but to make your cats share a toilet, just remember to keep the set-up clean at all times—flush as soon as you can after each use, and clean out the roasting pan if it's dirty. The last thing you want is to have a cat pooping in the hallway because another cat's poop is in the roasting pan!

A good way to keep track of your cats and bring some order to the toilet training process is to set a predefined potty time that's tied to their feeding schedule—for example, before mealtime when you first get up in the morning, or after their dinnertime (which works well if your cats like to use the bathroom right after a meal). When it's potty time, bring all of your cats and a big bag of treats into the bathroom and wait for them to use the toilet. When one of them does #1 and #2 successfully, praise and treat that cat (and because they're all together, this has the added benefit of showing the other cats that using the toilet results in a treat). If you repeat this ritual every day, your cats will eventually catch on that it's time for potty and treats, and with any luck, the cat who's making the fastest progress will show the slower cat(s) the way, leading by example. You'll also be present to clean and flush the toilet after each use.

You can only progress as quickly as the slowest cat will allow. Some cats will pick up toilet training faster than others; make sure you move at the pace of your slowest cat so that she doesn't get left behind.

Training a New Cat When There's Already a Toilet Trained Cat in the House

No matter how much cats fight, there always seems to be plenty of kittens.

—ABRAHAM LINCOLN

Introducing a new cat into your home can be tricky if other cats already occupy your house. It varies with each cat's personality, but their territorial instincts and personality conflicts can sometimes lead to fights, injuries, and a generally less-than-peaceful home. Successfully getting two strange cats to co-exist

Figure 24 *Cats are territorial, and getting two of them to co-exist peacefully can be a challenge*

peacefully is beyond the scope of this book, but if you plan on getting a new cat, I recommend that you read up on the topic, as well as speak with your breeder or vet before doing so.   One thing I *will* mention is that, if you're in the middle of toilet training a cat, you shouldn't bring a new animal into the house until your current cat is completely trained and has been for some time—the resultant stress of a new four-legged friend in the house can wreak havoc on her training progress.

When bringing a new, un-toilet trained cat into your home, the problem, of course, is that she needs a litter box. And once your trained cat notices the litter box, you can say goodbye to all the toilet training progress she's made—unless a cat has been toilet trained for a long time, given the choice between litter and the toilet, most cats will pick the litter.

You have two options:

1. Keep the cats separated until the new cat is toilet trained; or,
2. Let your trained cat regress, and re-train her while you train the new cat at the same time.

Separating the cats

If you have enough space and toilets available, you can keep the cats apart in their own separate areas of the house while you toilet train your new kitty. This way, you can prevent the trained cat from having access to any litter boxes or roasting pans that your new cat is learning on.

Of course, for this you'll need more than one toilet—one for training your new cat, and another for your trained cat to use.

Letting your trained cat regress, then re-training her

With all the painstaking progress you've made with toilet training your kitty, it might be tough for you to see your cat go back to using a roasting pan full of litter... but it might be easier to re-train than you think. It's sort of like taking an extended break from training; your cat already knows how to use the toilet, so she'll quickly pick it up again. And she might even lead the way in showing your new cat how it's done. If you don't have two toilets or you're unable to keep the two cats separated, this is the only way that you're going to be able to get the new cat toilet trained.

❽

Warning Signs

If animals could speak the dog would be a blundering
outspoken fellow, but the cat would have the rare grace
of never saying a word too much.
—MARK TWAIN, American humorist, writer and lecturer

Meow is like aloha—it can mean anything.
—HANK KETCHUM, creator of *Dennis the Menace*

We can't always expect your cat to vocalize her issues, so it's
important to watch for signs that she's uncomfortable with
the pace of progress, and to know when to slow down to give her
more time to adjust. By ignoring the warning signs, you run the
risk of bathroom accidents, as well as the risk of an unhealthy
cat. Some warning signs are obvious, and some are not so obvious. Here's what you need to watch out for.

Hesitation

No matter what stage of toilet training you're at, it's best to proceed to the next stage only when your cat stops showing signs of hesitation. If your cat is meowing incessantly before going to the toilet, pawing around the toilet area for an extended period of time, and generally dilly dallying at length before using the toilet, it's a good bet that she's not ready to proceed to the next stage, even if she's successfully using the current set-up. You'll need to give her more time to get used to whatever stage she's at before moving forward.

Toilet Avoidance

Most cats go #1 multiple times each day, and #2 about once a day. Kittens aged about 6 months and under will go #2 several times a day. You've monitored your cat's regular bathroom schedule like we discussed earlier, so you know how often your particular kitty goes; compare that with how frequently she goes during the course of her toilet training.

If you notice your cat going to the bathroom less often (and there's a very good chance that this will happen), don't panic; it's normal for her to be a *little* hesitant with an unfamiliar bathroom set-up. Cats can hold in their pee for 24 hours and poop for over 48 hours, and while that's not what we want to see happen, it's nothing to be alarmed about, as long as she doesn't consistently hold it in over a prolonged period of time. It does indicate, however, that she's not totally comfortable with the current set-up, so leave it alone for a few days. Chances are she'll eventually get used to it and will start using it more regularly, at which point you can proceed to the next stage of training.

Constipation Symptoms

Given a healthy diet and proper hydration, your cat shouldn't get constipated. Nevertheless, you should keep a close eye on her to ensure that her toilet avoidance doesn't get to this point. Symptoms to look out for include: straining unsuccessfully to pass feces, meowing in pain when trying to go, hard and dry stools, and even diarrhea. Other signs include lethargy, loss of appetite, and vomiting. If your cat exhibits these symptoms, take her to the vet—an examination will likely reveal a full bowel.

Constipation Prevention and Remedies

First off, make sure you are feeding your cat a healthy diet of canned wet food, not dry food, as discussed previously. Wet food will go a long way to ensuring sufficient hydration and preventing constipation. Also, remember that the best kind of wet foods are the quality brands that contain no by-products, excess corn, or starchy fillers.

If your cat *is* constipated, a little bit of fiber might go a long way. Try mixing a teaspoon or two of pumpkin into her food— either the canned or frozen variety, as mentioned previously. There are also commercially available laxatives such as Laxatone, Petromalt, and Furlax. Just remember to use these products sparingly, and not as part of her regular diet.

If your constipated cat is a lazy couch potato, try exercising your cat—this will help to stimulate her intestines and keep things moving. Play with her using her favorite toy, a feather, a laser pointer, etc... whatever it takes to get her running around the house.

Taking Breaks From Training

If your cat regularly holds it in for more than 48 hours at a time over a 7-day period or more, it's a good bet that she's backed up, even if she's not exhibiting any constipation symptoms. If this is the case with your cat, then take a break from training: give her the litter box back for a day or two and let her unconstipate herself before resuming.

Learning a new skill is tough, and even the best of us need a break now and then!

Taking Extended Breaks

Even if you go on an extended vacation, it's easy to resume toilet training when you get back. Don't worry about your cat forgetting about her toilet training or feel like you're undoing the progress that you and your cat have made—as much as your kitty dislikes change, she's an adaptable creature and will easily pick up where you left off.

To give you an example, I once gave a cat that I was potty training a two-month break from training while her owner was on vacation. This was when we were well into Stage 4 (the hole in the roasting pan had been enlarged to the point where more than half the bottom of the pan had been cut out). When we resumed training, we gave her one day to get reacquainted with the toilet by putting a roasting pan full of litter in it. After she successfully used the toilet once, we quickly moved on to having a hole in half the roasting pan again. The cat didn't miss a beat.

Keep your cat in good health—if you know that she's backed up, give her a break!

⑨

Correcting Accidents and Undesirable Behaviors

After scolding one's cat one looks into its face and is seized by the ugly suspicion that it understood every word. And has filed it for reference.
—CHARLOTTE GRAY, English-born Canadian journalist and historian

There's a fairly good chance that your cat will have an accident or three during the course of her toilet training. Whether it's because she doesn't know how to deal with the new bathroom set-up, or because she's rebelling and laying a "protest poop", here's what you need to know to handle the situation.

First and Foremost: Be Calm

Don't get upset or angry if your cat has an accident. Believe me, I know how tough it is to remain calm after discovering that kitty's just peed on the bathmat—not only is it disgusting, but you feel like you've failed in your toilet training. Resist your first instinct to take it out on the cat; there's a good chance that she feels bad enough about it already, being as prideful as she is.

Correct and Redirect

Instead of scolding and punishing the cat, we want to teach and correct her. Pick her up gently and take her over to the mess. Bring her about a foot from it so that she can smell it and, in a calm but firm voice, tell her "No!" Remember, it's completely mortifying for her to come face-to-face with her ripe excrement, so don't force her too close or rub her nose in it.

If it's a stool accident, then take the opportunity to show your cat where it belongs. Make sure your cat is in the bathroom with you when you put the waste in the toilet, praising her all the while as if she did it right to begin with. If your cat is visibly embarrassed, scared or upset, spend some time with her in the bathroom and reassure her that everything's all right and that you still love her. Once she's out of her doldrums, flush the toilet and praise her some more to show her that poops in the toilet is a good thing.

Backtrack Your Progress

A bathroom accident is a sure sign that you're moving just a little too fast for your cat's liking. Backtrack a step—go back to the previous stage, and give her more time to get used to it before proceeding further.

Clean The Mess

Make sure to thoroughly clean the area where the accident occurred. If the scent remains, your cat might think it's an appropriate place to go again, since she's gone there once before! Use an enzyme cleaner such as Nature's Miracle or Bio-Aid, then do a smell check. If there's a lingering smell but no stain, a black light can help you locate the affected area. If you've eliminated the smell with an enzyme cleaner but the stain is still there, you can try a regular cleaner to remove it (but only after you've used the enzyme cleaner; the chemicals in regular cleaners may react negatively with enzyme cleaners and prevent it from being effective).

Prevention

Of course, it's better to avoid bathroom accidents altogether. Besides monitoring your cat's comfort level and going slowly with the training, there are preventative measures that we can take to limit the chances of an accident occurring.

With all the changes to her bathroom routine, there are bound to be stages that she'll have difficulty with, and this is when she'll be tempted to find someplace easier to go. You can usually predict where the accidents will be, too: in corners of rooms, in plants, on bathmats, on piles of dirty laundry, and basically anything that's absorbent and hidden away. So, if your kitty is having potty issues at a certain stage and is in danger of having an accident, remove these temptations to help make the toilet the most inviting place to do her business.

- Make sure you don't keep towels or piles of laundry on the floor. If you have a bathmat, hang it up after you're done showering.

- Try to keep your cat out of the bedroom as much as possible. When you're out of the house, keep the bedroom door closed, so she isn't given the chance to do her business on your bed sheets.

- You can restrict your cat's space even further by locking her in her bathroom when you're sleeping or away from the house. Your cat is more likely to use the toilet set-up if they don't have access to beds, rugs, and other areas of the house that may be tempting to pee or poop on. Even if they go on the floor of the bathroom, it's much easier to clean the floor than it is to clean fabrics.

- For large houseplants, cover the dirt as much as you can with aluminum foil or duct tape, so your cat isn't tempted to squat in the pot or dig up the dirt to use as litter. Best way to do this is to use duct tape with the sticky side up, since cats usually dislike the texture of anything that's sticky.

- If your cat decides the sink or the bathtub is a good place to defecate, try keeping it filled with an inch of water. For a sink, you can also try leaving an empty shampoo bottle in it. The idea is to set up obstacles in these places to make the toilet seem like a more attractive place to go by comparison.

You can also make the toilet set-up more appealing by changing the litter frequently during the stages where litter is involved. Cats like things to be extremely clean and prefer fresh, clean litter over used litter 100% of the time, so make the toilet training set-up more appealing by always having fresh litter in the roasting pan.

Speaking of Accidents in Absorbent Places...

I can confidently say that I've endured one of the more spectacular bathroom accidents in kitty toilet training history. Hopefully, after learning about the tips and techniques in this book, nothing like this will happen to you.... Consider the following a precautionary tale.

When I was toilet training Miki, I was fairly careful to remove any absorbent materials off the floor, including bathmats, towels, and laundry. Unfortunately, there was one thing that I forgot—an umbrella, which I'd absent-mindedly left on the floor of the hallway entry for a few days. This was a small folding umbrella that collapsed in half when closed, and I had left it standing neatly upright on the floor, untied and splayed open like some giant, liquid-absorbing bucket. You can guess what happened next....

One afternoon, Miki started meowing incessantly and seemed extremely agitated—I'd never heard anything like it from her before. Suspecting that she'd had an accident, I searched the usual places for signs of pee or poop—the bathmat, the potted plant, corners of rooms—but found nothing. So, I chalked it up to the cat just being in one of her crazy moods.

The next day, however, as my fiancée rushes out of the house to get to school, she grabs the umbrella on her way out the door and—you guessed it—cat pee flies everywhere.

Conveniently, while all this is happening, I'm sitting in the coffee shop down the block from our apartment, quietly enjoying a cup of joe. I get a frantic call from my poor fiancée and immediately rush home to console her; she's forced to skip class, and we spend the rest of the morning cleaning up the hallway. Needless to say, we also throw the umbrella in the trash, as well as two pairs of her shoes that were caught in the line of fire.

Moral of the story: if your cat is having difficulty with some stage of toilet training, make sure you don't leave any large, absorbent, bucket-shaped objects lying on the floor.

A final word on accidents: I know it's natural to feel bad for your cat when she appears to dislike the training process, but just remember—learning *any* new skill is difficult, and if you just give her enough time to get used to the human toilet, it *will* eventually become second nature to her. Also, remember that training can be a rewarding experience for both trainer and trainee; cats are certainly capable of feeling a sense of pride for a job well done. I'm sure your cat enjoys all the treats and praise you lavish upon her, too!

Undesirable Behaviors

I found out why cats drink out of the toilet. My mother
told me it's because the water is cold in there. And I'm
like: How did my mother know that?
—WENDY LIEBMAN, comedian

Here are some of the more common behaviors your cat might exhibit that can put a damper on her toilet training, and what you can do about it.

Drinking Out of the Toilet

Cats love fresh, cool water, so don't be surprised if your cat likes to drink out of the toilet, since the water in the toilet bowl is changed every time it's flushed. You can discourage this behavior by putting a little bit of vinegar in the toilet after every flush.

Try not to scold her or correct her by saying "No," since she might just get confused and think that everything to do with the toilet is a no-no, and end up staying away from the toilet entirely!

Fortunately, this problem usually goes away on its own after your cat starts using the toilet for its intended purpose, since cats generally don't like to eat and drink in the same place where they defecate.

Digging Inside the Toilet Bowl

The instinct to dig is particularly strong in some cats, and yours might be inclined to "dig" the water in the toilet bowl after she's gone #1 or #2—a pretty disgusting habit! If your cat attempts to paw at the water after she's used the toilet, you can discourage this behavior by calling her away from the toilet immediately after she's finished, and rewarding her with a treat. With enough repetition, this will help condition your cat to forget about burying her waste after she does her business, even when you're not around to supervise.

Playing With the Toilet Paper

While your cat is on the toilet seat, she might be inclined to destroy any rolls of toilet paper that are nearby, creating a mess of TP in your bathroom. Some cats will do this to attempt to cover up their waste, using the toilet paper as if it were litter. Other cats will do this just because it's fun. To prevent it from happening, just turn the toilet paper roll around so that the paper comes out from under the roll; this way, it won't unravel easily if she paws it.

⑩

Alternate Toilet Training Methods

There are always alternatives.
—SPOCK, *Star Trek*

There are a number of other methods for toilet training cats, and I've tried all of these, with varying degrees of success. The underlying principles—such as keeping the toilet seat down, proper diet, and giving praise—still apply to these methods; the main difference is using an alternative training apparatus other than a roasting pan. These include:

- Saran wrap
- Wax paper
- A mixing bowl
- A sitz bath
- Commercially available contraptions

Your toilet training education wouldn't be entirely complete without at least a bit of knowledge of these commonly used approaches, so I'll go over each briefly. There are advantages and disadvantages to each, and if nothing else, they present some interesting considerations for toilet training.

The Saran Wrap / Wax Paper Method

With this method, instead of putting a roasting pan in the toilet for your kitty to use as her litter box, you simply cover the toilet bowl with saran wrap or wax paper to create a barrier (and tape it down to secure it if necessary). Then, put down the toilet seat, and sprinkle some litter over the barrier. After your cat gets used this set-up, poke a hole in the middle of the barrier, exposing the water in the toilet bowl. As your cat grows accustomed to doing her business this way, gradually enlarge the hole until eventually there's nothing left of the saran wrap / wax paper.

Advantages of saran wrap / wax paper

The advantage of saran wrap is that, since saran wrap is clear, your cat can get used to seeing the water beneath her in the beginning, before you poke that hole in the saran wrap and expose it. This makes the transition to water a lot less scary for her.

Disadvantages of saran wrap / wax paper

The basic idea of this method is to make your cat feel insecure enough about sitting in the saran wrap / wax paper that she'll stand on the toilet seat instead. (Saran wrap and wax paper typically aren't strong enough to support a cat's weight, especially when a hole has been poked in the middle of it... and even assuming that your cat's weight can be supported, your cat won't like it when the saran wrap or wax paper gives like a trampoline.)

Unfortunately, what usually happens is that your cat decides that the floor is an even more secure place to do her business.

Moreover, you're limited in how much litter you can put on top of the barrier, and much of it will probably end up on the floor as well. You also won't be able to construct a litter dam to prevent litter from falling into the toilet.

This method is also only practical if you have a spare toilet to devote to the cat—it's rather inconvenient to disassemble and reassemble the saran wrap / wax paper and litter set-up each time someone needs to use the bathroom.

The Mixing Bowl Method

With this method, you'll need to procure a metal mixing bowl that will fit snuggly in your toilet bowl. Fill the mixing bowl with an inch or two of litter, and give kitty some time to get comfortable using it as her litter box.

Your cat will likely begin by placing her front paws on the toilet seat, hind legs in the mixing bowl. At this point, you'll need to teach her proper paw position as described earlier (Stage 4 of our regular process), with the goal of getting her to put all four paws on the toilet seat.

Once your cat uses the toilet regularly with all four paws on the seat, begin reducing the amount of litter inside the mixing bowl, and keep doing this until your cat is peeing and pooping into the bowl with no litter. You'll need to be present to clean out the mixing bowl immediately after your cat uses it each time, because the odor's going to be unbearable for both you and your cat, especially as the litter gets low—you'll want to get rid of it quickly.

Now that your cat is peeing and pooping sans litter, add a bit of water to the mixing bowl to introduce her to the idea of going in water.　Gradually increase the amount of water in the bowl each time she does her business until there's about two inches of water in the bowl.　Once your cat has reached this stage, remove the mixing bowl completely, leaving the bare toilet.

Advantages of a mixing bowl

A mixing bowl stuffed snuggly in the toilet provides a very secure place for kitty to do her business—it's solid and doesn't shift around, so kitty feels nice and secure.　(Just don't use a plastic bowl that won't support her weight!)

A mixing bowl is also easy to remove from the toilet, in case any humans want to use the toilet during kitty's training.　The same cannot be said of the saran wrap / wax paper method.

Disadvantages of a mixing bowl

One of the toughest aspects of this method that make it rather impractical is that it requires you to be present almost all of the time.　For starters, you'll need to be around to teach your cat proper paw position—a mixing bowl is very deep, so much so that it's nearly impossible for your cat to learn proper paw position on her own.　You'll definitely need to make the effort to teach her.

As well, because your cat will be doing her business in an empty mixing bowl without litter, you'll need to be present so that you can clean out the mixing bowl right after she's done; otherwise, your cat will be faced with the prospect of dealing with her own ripe excrement without any litter.　It would be very easy to traumatize your cat and discourage her from using the toilet!

Where most cats really run into trouble, though, is when water is introduced to the equation.　You may be able to convince your cat to go into the empty mixing bowl once or twice, but the instant you add water to the bowl, she'll balk and refuse to use the set-up. Even if you try to start off slowly and only add a tiny bit of water, the water, combined with the fact that there's no litter, is just too much for most cats to handle... it's the proverbial straw that breaks the camel's back.

Finally, a new mixing bowl is simply more expensive than our other options... and believe me, you're not going to want to re-use it for cooking after you've finished toilet training your cat with it!

The Sitz Bath Method

A sitz bath is a plastic tub that sits over the toilet. Its intended purpose is to allow humans to sit in warm water, helping to heal and ease discomfort of ailments that affect that part of the body... as it turns out, though, it can also be used to teach cats how to use the toilet. The method is the same as the roasting pan method, except that the sitz bath is used instead of the aluminum pan. When it's time to expose the water, you cut a round hole in the middle of the sitz bath, gradually enlarging it as your cat progresses.

Advantages of a sitz bath

The sitz bath is designed to fit inside a toilet, so it's guaranteed to be snug and secure. It's also made of plastic, so a good quality sitz bath can do a better job of supporting your cat's weight than an aluminum roasting pan.

Disadvantages of a sitz bath

Because the sitz bath is made of plastic, it's much harder to cut than aluminum; you'll need more than a regular pair of scissors to do the job. Similarly, it's not possible to shape a litter dam out of the plastic; to make a litter dam, you'll need to glue some-thing to the sitz bath create a fence around the hole. For exam-ple, if you cut a round hole in the middle of the sitz bath, you could fashion a dam by gluing an empty toilet paper roll or cardboard tube on top of the hole, creating a tunnel of sorts from the top of the sitz bath to the water below. As you can imagine, it's a lot of work to cut away the plastic and build a new litter dam every time you wanted to expand the hole. Not only that, but if you make a mistake in cutting the hole or need to backtrack a step or two, it would get expensive with a sitz bath, whereas a new roasting pan is only a couple of dollars.

Commercial Kits

There are commercially available kits out there that are designed for toilet training your cat. I won't waste too many trees talking about them here; a quick search on Google will reveal more about them. Most of them work like a plastic roasting pan or a sitz bath, but they have pre-defined rings that you either pop off or cut out to gradually enlarge the hole.

Advantages of a commercial kit

Like a sitz bath, a commercial kit is specifically designed for a toilet, so fit should not be a problem. Also, some kits don't re-quire you to do any cutting, which saves you the effort of having to cut a roasting pan.

Disadvantages of a commercial kit

Some commercial kits are sturdy, some are not. The ones that aren't are made with flimsy plastic that bend under a cat's weight (especially if she's on the heavy side), making the toilet training process scary and potentially traumatic for the poor cat.

If your cat ever fell into the toilet because the contraption couldn't support her weight—and I've known this to happen—it would probably set your training back weeks, if not months!

In addition, because the commercial devices have pre-defined ring sizes, it means you have very limited flexibility in how large you want the holes to be. Commercial kits force your cat to adapt in 3-4 steps. Many cats balk when the first hole is made, simply because it's too big and it's right in the middle of the device. Likewise, many cats have problems giving up the last ring because it's too big a step for them.

And of course, there's cost—commercial toilet training devices generally aren't cheap. Some also require you to cut a hole in the plastic, which makes it impossible to backtrack if you need to. There are better ones available that are designed in such a way that allow you to backtrack, but those are also generally more expensive.

Appendix: Resources Discussed In This Book

Products

Flushable Litter

Most brands of flushable litter will work just fine for toilet training—the most important thing is that your cat accepts the litter and actually uses it. Try to avoid crystal litters as they make a "sizzling" sound when put in water, which may disturb your cat whilst she's trying to do her business.

The litters listed below are excellent brands that are flushable, dust-free, and clump well.

➤**World's Best Cat Litter**
http://www.worldsbestcatlitter.com

➤**Swheat Scoop**
http://www.swheatscoop.com

Canned Wet Foods

Both of these brands are complete, balanced diets that can be served on a daily basis as your cat's sole diet.

➤**Nature's Variety® Instinct™**
http://www.naturesvariety.com

➤**Wellness® Canned Cat Food**
http://www.wellnesspetfood.com

Laxatives

➤**Laxatone™**
http://www.tomlyn.com

➤**Petromalt®**
http://www.virbacpets.com/petromalt/

Nutrition Information

Interested in improving your cat's health and well-being? Check out the following resources—they are great starting points for learning more about feline nutrition.

➤**Canned Cat Food Nutrition Information (contains a breakdown of the nutritional content in popular brands of cat food)**
http://www.geocities.com/jmpeerson/canfood.html

➤**A list of quality cat foods at Consumer Search**

http://www.consumersearch.com/www/family/cat-food/review.html

➤The "Catkins" Diet
http://www.catnutrition.org/catkins.php

➤ "Grains in the Feline Diet." *Feline Future*
http://www.felinefuture.com/nutrition/grains.php

➤Lisa A. Pierson (DVM). "Feeding Your Cat: Know the Basics of Feline Nutrition." *CatInfo.org*
http://www.catinfo.org/

➤Jean Hofve (DVM). "Does Dry Food Clean the Teeth?" *Little Big Cat*
http://www.littlebigcat.com/index.php?action=library&act=show&item=doesdryfoodcleantheteeth

➤Edmund R. Dorosz (BSA, DVM). "What Is Best, Cooked Or Raw?" *NetPets.com*
http://www.netpets.com/cats/reference/food/cookorraw.html

➤Fraser A. Hale (DVM, DAVDC). "Home Care for Prevention of Periodontal Disease in Dogs and Cats." *Proceedings of the 2006 Hill's NAVC & WVC Symposiums*
http://www.cliniciansbrief.com/cms/portals/_default/pdfs/other-publications/Hills%2005%20Pro%20Fnl_TOCetc.pdf

➤Michael S. Hand, P Roudebush, CD Thatcher, RL Remillard. *Small Animal Clinical Nutrition 4th edition.* Walsworth Publishing Company. Marceline, MO; 2000

Index

➤About the Author

Aston Lau (aka "The Poo Whisperer" to his friends) has a degree in Computer Science and a minor in English from the University of British Columbia. He has worked as a programmer, project manager, designer, and writer. He is also a cat lover who really dislikes scooping the litter box. He currently lives in Vancouver, British Columbia.

➤About the Cat

Besides being fully toilet trained, Miki the Cat is also an expert eater and catnapper. Now an indoor cat, in her previous life she was a neglected "office cat" who roamed the streets of Vancouver's Gastown district before being adopted by Aston and his fiancée. She takes great pride in being able to use the regular toilet like a human.

11801698R1008

Made in the USA
Lexington, KY
02 November 2011